地獄草紙

詞書

全文翻刻・解読
現代日本語訳
英訳

マシュー・スタブロス　監修・翻訳
ジェマイマ・ライス　英文校訂

Hell Scrolls

A complete transcription and translation of
Jigokuzōshi, the *Hell Scrolls* in the collections of
the Nara National Museum and the Tokyo National
Museum, including a fragment from the Nara Scroll
in the collection of the Museum of Fine Arts,
Boston.

Edited, transcribed, and translated into
Modern Japanese and English by
Matthew Stavros, Ph.D.

With editorial collaboration from
Jemima Rice

Vicus Lusorum
2025

目次

凡例・書誌 iv

Introduction and Conventions viii

奈良本『地獄草紙』Nara Hell Scroll 1

  第一段　屎糞所 The Sub-Hell of Excrement 6

  第二段　函量所 The Sub-Hell of Crooked Measurements ... 10

  第三段　鉄磑所 The Sub-Hell of the Iron Mortar 14

  第四段　鶏身雞 The Sub-Hell of the Flaming Rooster ... 18

黒雲沙処 　The Sub-Hell of Black Sand Clouds	22
膿血処 　The Sub-Hell of Pus and Blood	26
ボストン美術館蔵『辟邪絵』MFA, Boston Fragment	
一鑊湯処 　The Sub-Hell of One Copper Cauldron	27
単輪本『辟邪絵』Tokyo Hell Scroll	
第一紙　髪火流処 　The Sub-Hell of Flaming Torrents of Hair	31
第二紙　火末虫処 　The Sub-Hell of Insects at the Tips of Flames	36
第三紙　雲火霧処 　The Sub-Hell of Cloud-Fire Mist	40
第四紙　雨炎火石処 　The Sub-Hell of Flaming Rain and Rocks	44
	48

v

前書き・凡例

本書は、十二世紀に成立した重要な絵画史料『地獄草紙』を活字化し、初心者から研究者まで幅広く活用できる参考文献を提供することを目的としている。奈良国立博物館所蔵の『地獄草紙』（今後「奈博本」）と東京国立博物館所蔵の『地獄草紙』（東博本）の二点の国宝に加え、ボストン美術館所蔵の奈博本断簡一通に記された各段の詞書（銘文）を、四通りの方法で書き起こした。

まず、各詞書（銘文）を可能な限り原文のまま忠実にテキスト化した。旧字体・異体字・変体仮名、歴史的仮名遣いなどを修正せず、改行箇所も原文どおりとし、ルビも付していない。

二つ目は解読文である。解読文では、原文に対して以下の点に配慮した。

- 旧字体・異体字・変体仮名を現代の字体に置き換えた
- 歴史的仮名遣いにはルビを付した
- 濁音として読まれる箇所には濁点を付し、句読点も補った
- 読み仮名は、研究者の間で一般的とされる読みを採用した
- 改行箇所は原文のままとした

vi

さらに、現代日本語訳と英訳も付した。原文の文脈と意味を尊重しつつ、理解しやすい平易な日本語と英語で表現することを心がけた。両訳には注釈を加え、内容の理解を補う参考情報を記した。

『地獄草紙』の詳細については、以下の代表的な文献を参照されたい。

- 小松茂美（編集・解説）『日本の絵巻』第七巻「餓鬼草紙　地獄草紙　病草紙　九相詩絵巻」、中央公論社、1987年。
- 山本聡美『中世仏教絵画の図像誌』吉川弘文館、2020年。
- 小松茂美『日本絵巻聚稿』第一巻、中央公論社、1986年。

『地獄草紙』に関する追加情報や資料、高解像度画像データを掲載した本書の伴侶サイトを公開している。
www.vicuslusorum.com/hungry-ghosts

また、『地獄草紙』の高画質画像データは emuseum.nich.go.jp でも閲覧可能である。

vii

Introduction and Conventions

This reference work includes complete transcriptions and translations of the inscriptions that appear in *Jigokuzōshi*, the *Hell Scrolls* in the collections of the Nara National Museum and the Tokyo National Museum. Both date to the 12th century and are registered Japanese national treasures. A fragment from the Nara Scroll in the collection of the Museum of Fine Arts, Boston is also included.

Each inscription is presented in four formats:
- Exact Transcription (*honkoku*): A transcription of the primary text exactly as it appears in the original document, including archaic scripts (historical *kana*, *kyūjitai*, and *itaiji*). No changes or corrections have been made, and no punctuation marks have been added;
- Accessible Version (*kaidokubun*): The grammar and syntax of the primary text have been maintained, but archaic scripts have been replaced by modern equivalents. Phonetic guides (*furigana*) and punctuation marks have been added to facilitate reading;
- Modern Japanese Translation: A direct translation of the primary text into modern Japanese. Translations have not been embellished to enhance lyricism, however, notes have been added to improve clarity;
- English Translation: A direct translation of the primary text into English. Translations have not been embellished to enhance lyricism, however, notes have been added to improve clarity.

As a work of reference, this book does not provide detailed information on the historical or cultural significance of the scrolls. Readers are encouraged to see these representative works in English:
- Caroline Hirasawa, "The Inflatable, Collapsible Kingdom of Retribution: A Primer on Japanese Hell Imagery and Imagination." *Monumenta Nipponica*, vol. 63, no. 1, Spring 2008: 1-50.

- Satomi Yamamoto, "Death and Disease in Medieval Japanese Painting." *Treatises and studies by the Faculty of Kinjo Gakuin College*, vol. 6, no. 2, 2010: 81-96. (kinjo. repo.nii.ac.jp/record/222/files/KJ00006279600.pdf)
- Anna Willmann, "Japanese Illustrated Handscrolls." The Metropolitan Museum of Art, New York. (www.metmuseum. org/essays/japanese-illustrated-handscrolls)

A companion website is accessible at www.vicus lusorum.com/hell-scrolls and high resolution versions of the Nara and Tokyo scrolls can be viewed at emuseum.nich.go.jp.

奈良国立博物館所蔵（奈博本）

『地獄草紙』詞書

奈博本　第1段　屎糞所（しふんしょ）　原文翻刻

まつ別所ありなをハ屎糞所と
いふむかし人とありしときにうる
をろかにしてきよからぬ物を
きよしとおもひきたなからぬ
をのをきたなしとおもひ佛法
にあなから三寶をうやまふ
心なきをけこの地獄にをくの
あなれふかきにをちいるつミ人
乃くにたつろのくかのかれくさ
くけからはしきたとくむかたなを
ふのなか　針口
罪人をハみくらふ苦患たえかたを

奈博本　第1段　屎糞所(しふんしょ)　解読文

また別所(べっしょ)あり。名をば屎糞所と
いふ。昔(むかし)、人とあリし時、心
愚(おろ)かにして、清(きよ)からぬ物を
清しと思ひ、汚(きたな)からぬ
物を汚(きたな)しと思ひ、仏法(ぶっぽう)
に合(あ)ひながら三宝(さんぼう)を敬(うやま)ふ
心なき者(もの)、この地獄(じごく)に堕(お)つ。糞(くそ)の
穴(あな)の深(ふか)きに陥(お)ちいる罪人(つみびと)
の首に立つその糞(くそ)の香(か)の臭(くさ)
く、汚(けが)らはしきこと、例(たと)へむ方(かた)な無(な)し。
その中(なか)(に)カ　針口(しんく)(無数)カ、
罪人を食(は)み食(く)らふ。苦(くる)しき、耐(た)えがたし。

奈博本 第一段 屎糞所(しふんしょ) 現代語訳

もう一つの別所(べっしょ)がある。その名を屎糞所という。昔、人間であった時、心が愚(おろ)かで、清(きよ)くない物を清いと思い、汚(きたな)くない物を汚いと思い、また仏法(ぶっぽう)に従(したが)いながら三宝(さんぼう)を尊敬(そんけい)する心ない者がこの地獄(じごく)に堕(お)ちる。

糞(くそ)の穴(あな)の深(ふか)い所に堕ちている罪人(つみびと)は糞の悪臭(あくしゅう)が首(くび)まで届(とど)き、その汚(けが)らわしさは、例(たと)えようがない。その穴の中に針口虫(しんくちゅう)がおり、罪人を齧(かじ)り食(く)う。苦患(くげん)は耐(た)えがたい。

* 『起世経(きせきょう)』によると八大地獄があり、その周辺に十六の「別所」という小地獄がある。
* 「三宝」とは、仏教において最も尊敬すべき三つのもの、仏・法・僧である。
* 『正法念処経(しょうぼうねんじょきょう)』によると「針口虫」は人の体内にいるという八十種の虫の一つである。梵語では Nyaṅkuṭā のことであろう。

Nara Scroll, Verse 1: The Sub-Hell of Excrement

There is yet another sub-hell*. As for its name, it is called "The [Sub-Hell] of Excrement." The ones who descend into this hell are those who, long ago, when they were human, were unwise; those who thought impure things were pure and unclean things were clean, and who did not have the fortitude to respect the Three Treasures† while following the Dharma.

Excrement comes up to the necks of those sinners who have fallen into the deepest part of the excrement pit. The stench and filth are incomparable. Maggots‡ gnaw away at the sinners in the pit. The agony is intolerable.

* Several Buddhist sutras identify eight "great hells" and 16 "sub-hells." A similar concept, called "*nakara*," is found in Hindu cosmology. All the verses in the Nara Scroll are inspired by descriptions of sub-hells in the *Sutra on the Origins of the World* (Jp. *Kise kyō*; Pali *Aggañña sutta*).
† The "Three Treasures" or "Three Jewels" in Buddhism include the Buddha, the Dharma, and the sangha. Practitioners are meant to "take refuge" in the three treasures.
‡ These bugs appear in the *Meditation on the Correct Teaching Sutra* (Jp. *Shōbō nen jo-kyō*) and are described as one of the 80 types of bugs that reside in the body. In Indian texts, they appear as nyaṅkuṭā.

奈博本　第一一段　函量所(かんりょうしょ)　原文翻刻

また別所あり名をば函量
所といふむかし人間もあるそ
ときはけふつけておうは
うをててみをなやましある
いはあきなひまつ人をなや
ましうたてかのしもをにの別所
ておきねこ乃といゝておゝあり
てふとけのうつねものをもちて
くろかねのたけくおにのと紹おき
たはみ人よをからすにとや
ますしてふまうしくつみの
おくらに

奈博本 第二段 函量所(かんりょうしょ) 解読文

また別所(べっしょ)あり。名(な)をば函量所(かんりょうしょ)といふ。昔、人間(にんげん)にありし時、斗升(とます)につけて横暴(おうぼう)し、民(たみ)を悩(なや)まし、或(ある)いは商(あきな)ひする人を悩(なや)まし、うたでがりし者、この別所に生(む)まる。この所に鬼(おに)ありて、ひとつの器物(うつわもの)をもちて、黒金(くろがね)の猛(たけ)く熾(おこ)りたる燠(おき)を罪人(ざいにん)に測(はか)らすこと止(や)まずして久(ひさ)しく[を脳力(のうりき)]苦(くる)しみ、忍(しの)ぶべからず。

奈博本 第二段 函量所(かんりょうしょ) 現代語訳

もう１つの別所がある。その名を函量所という。昔、人間であった時、斗升*を悪用し、民や商人を悩ませるような、嘆かわしかった人がこの別所に生まれる。

この所に鬼がいる。鬼は罪人に、１つの容器で猛烈に燃えている黒金の漿を休まず測らせる。長く続いている苦しみは忍ぶことができない。

* 「斗升」とは約18リットルの容量をはかる計量器のこと。前近代おいては主に米や酒、調味料などの計量に使用され、商売に不可欠な単位であった。

Nara Scroll, Verse 2: The Sub-Hell of Crooked Measurements

There is yet another sub-hell. As for its name, it is called "The [Sub-Hell] of [Crooked] Measurements." The ones born into this sub-hell are deplorable. They are those who, long ago, when they were human, harassed commoners and merchants by perverting the fundamental system of measurements*.

There are demons in this place. They make sinners use a single bowl to ceaselessly measure cinders of fiercely burning iron. Enduring such sustained suffering is impossible.

* The original text refers to the misuse of a *"tomasu,"* a fundamental unit of measure equivalent to a container of about 18 liters used to measure rice, sake, and seasonings. To misuse it would constitute a kind of commercial fraud or cheating.

奈博本　第三段　鉄鐙所(てつがいしよ)　原文翻刻

また別所ありなをは鐵鐙所(カイ)
といふむかし人のむまれしとき
にゝかてまし/\てひとの物を
すかしとりてものむくひもなく
あるはにゝるにゝうとまし
かりし人々の別所よむまるゝ乃
ところよ獄卒罪人をとりてくる
かねのすゝうすよいれて
うちまろはしてその身〳〵
さけちのいひへるしみたゝく
祓ゑるによものなを

奈博本　第三段　鉄礑所（てつがいしょ）解読文

また別所(べっしょ)あり。名(な)をば鉄礑所(てつがいしょ)といふ。昔、人に生(む)まれたりし時、心(ね)妬(ねた)ましくして、人の物(もの)を賺(すか)し取りて、その報(むく)ひもなく、或(ある)いは、心(に)憎(にく)く疎(うと)ましかりし人、この別所に生(む)まる。この所に獄卒(ごくそつ)、罪人(つみびと)を取りて、黒(くろ)き金(かね)の磨(す)る臼(うす)に入れて頻(しき)りに磨(す)り拉(ひし)ぐ。その身(み)分(ぶん)、譬(たと)へば砕(くだ)け散(ち)る。痛(いた)み苦(くる)しみ、譬(たと)へを取るに物なし。

奈博本 第三段 鉄礑所(てつがいしょ) 現代語訳

もう一つの別所(べっしょ)がある。その名を鉄礑所という。昔、人間として生まれてきた時、心が妬(ねた)ましく、他人の物を騙(だま)し取っても報(むく)いのない人、或いは心憎(にく)く疎(うと)ましかった人がこの別所に生まれる。

この所に地獄の鬼が罪人を捕(つか)まえ、黒金(くろがね)の磨(す)り白(うす)に入れ、頻(しき)りに磨(す)り潰(つぶ)す。罪人の身体(からだ)は砕(くだ)け散(ち)る。その痛(いた)みや苦(くる)しみを譬(たと)える物はない。

Nara Scroll, Verse 3: The Sub-Hell of the Iron Mortar

There is yet another sub-hell. As for its name, it is called "The [Sub-Hell] of the Iron Mortar." The ones born into this sub-hell are those who, long ago, when they had been born human, were jealous; they tricked and robbed people of their things without compunction, and were hateful and detestable people.

In this place, the demons of hell snatch sinners, put them into an iron mortar and grind them incessantly. The sinners' bodies are pulverized to bits. The pain and suffering has no equivalent.

奈博本　第四段　鶏地獄（にわとりじごく）　原文翻刻

またこの地獄に別所あり鶏地
獄となつくむかし人間にありし
ときにゝわとおろかなるによりては
らあしくして諸さかをこ
のみあるいはいけるものをころ
めとりけたものをなやますもの
これにむまるこの地獄にたけき
ほのほ身にみちたるにはとりありて
罪人をしきりに蹴りふむ罪人の
身分つたゝにになりてその苦患た
えをのふくきかたなき

奈博本　第四段　鶏地獄(にわとりじごく)　解読文

またこの地獄に別所あり。鶏地獄と名づく。昔、人間にありし時、心愚(おろ)かなるによりて、腹悪(はらあ)しくして、静(しずか)ひを好(この)み、或(ある)いは、生けるものを侘(わ)びしめ、鳥・獣(けだもの)を悩(なや)ます者(もの)、これに生まる。この地獄に猛(たけ)き炎(ほのお)、身に満みちたる鶏(にわとり)ありて、罪人を頻(しき)りに蹴(け)り踏む。罪人の身分(みぶん)づたづたになりて、その苦患(くげん)耐(た)え忍(しの)ぶべき方(かた)なし。

奈博本　第四段　鶏地獄（にわとりじごく）　現代語訳

この地獄に、もう一つの別所がある。鶏地獄と名付ける。昔、人間であった時、心が愚かである故、腹黒くて喧嘩を好む人、或いは生き物を困らせ、鳥や獣を悩ませる者がこの別所に生まれる。

この地獄に身体が猛烈な炎に満ちた鶏がおり、その鶏が罪人を頻りに蹴り踏む。罪人の身体はずたずたになり、その苦患は耐え忍ぶことができない。

Nara Scroll, Verse 4: The Sub-Hell of the Flaming Rooster

In this hell, there is yet another sub-hell. It is named "The [Sub-Hell] of the [Flaming] Rooster." The ones born into this sub-hell are those who, long ago, when they were human, were wicked and liked to quarrel because they were unwise; and those who caused animals grief, tormenting birds and beasts.

In this hell is a rooster whose body is engulfed in fierce flames. The rooster kicks and stomps on sinners incessantly. The sinners' bodies are torn to shreds and there is no way for them to tolerate the agony.

奈博本　第五段　黒雲沙(こくうんしや)　原文翻刻

又た別所ありなをは黒雲沙と

いふむかしくとむまれていへる

にくヽあしくをてとをそいなひ

をとのひ息をやかむといへのみ

もれいのちいくてをついのとい

ろヽくるまくものかよりあけ

きらたいふりて罪人をやくい

とそとえ救その苦ひゆしくを

ぬきのらかたし

奈博本　第五段　黒雲沙（こくうんしゃ）　解読文

また別所あり。名をば黒雲沙といふ。昔、人と生まれて、心憎く悪しくして、[脳力]を損ない、人の家を焼かむと好みし者、この地獄に堕つ。この所に黒き雲の中より、熱き沙子降りて、罪人を焼くこと絶えず。その苦、久しくして忍び難し。

奈博本　第五段　黒雲沙（こくうんしゃ）　現代語訳

もう一つの別所がある。その名を黒雲沙という。昔、人として生まれ、心が憎く、人を損ない、家を焼こうとすることを好んだ者がこの地獄に堕ちる。

この所では、黒い雲の中より、熱い砂が降り、罪人を絶えず焼く。その苦しみは長く忍びがたい。

Nara Scroll, Verse 5: The Sub-Hell of Black Sand Clouds

There is yet another sub-hell. As for its name, it is called "The [Sub-Hell] of Black Sand Clouds." The ones who descend into this hell are those who, long ago, when they had been born human, were detestable and injurious to others; they are those who enjoyed trying to burn down houses.

In this place, hot sand rains down from black clouds, ceaselessly scalding the sinners. The suffering is difficult to tolerate for long.

奈博本　第六段　膿血所(のうけつしょ)　原文翻刻

また別所ありなをは膿血所と

いふおかしひとたのしとき𛂱ゝる

た𛃭かるをきてくてん𛁈𛂞𛀸

かぞらくろくまきをあきものを

人𛁚くをあつくしものこれ地獄

におちこのとひうちらみをるた

ほくそくくの𛁀がくして罪人

の𛁀ちをな𛀸をたくの𛁈𛂞𛀸𛂞

か最猛勝といふむしありて罪人を

くらふ𛂞ねとか𛁘のま𛁘ふ者

をつみ𛂱と𛁘くむか𛂱𛁀おゝ

奈博本　第六段　膿血所解読文

また別所あり。名をば膿血所という。昔、人たりし時、心愚かにして、すべて人のため に腹黒く、汚き物を人に食はせ与へし者、この地獄に堕つ。この所に膿血汁る多く湛へり、深くして、罪人の口・鼻に及べり。生臭に最猛勝という虫ありて、罪人を食らふ。骨通り、筋破れ、苦しみ例へむ方無し。

奈博本 第六段 膿血所(のうけつしょ) 現代語訳

もう一つの別所(べっしょ)がある。その名を膿血所という。この地獄に堕(お)ちるのは、昔、人であった時、心が愚(おろ)かで、すべての人に対して腹黒(はらぐろ)く、汚(きたな)い物を与(あた)えて食(く)わせた者(もの)である。

この所には多くの膿汁(うみじる)が溜(た)まっており、罪人(つみびと)の口や鼻(はな)まで深(ふか)く及(およ)んでいる。そこに、生臭(なまぐさ)い最猛勝(さいみょうしょう)*という虫がおり、罪人を食う。骨(ほね)を通(とお)り、筋(すじ)を破(やぶ)り、苦(くる)しみは例(たと)えようがない。

*「最猛勝」とは『起世経』第二巻に説かれている鉤状毛による翅の結合構造を持つ蜂のような虫である。

Nara Scroll, Verse 6: The Sub-Hell of Pus and Blood

There is yet another sub-hell. As for its name, it is called "The [Sub-Hell] of Pus and Blood." The ones who descend into this hell are those who, long ago, when they were human, were unwise; those who were malicious towards all people, giving them filth to eat.

A vast amount of puss pervades this place, rising right up to the mouths and noses of the sinners. There are insects that smells of raw flesh called *saimōshō** that eat the sinners. The bones of the sinners are penetrated, their sinew torn. The suffering is incomparable.

---

* *Saimyōshō* are mythical insects described in the second chapter of the *Sutra on the Origins of the World* (Jp. *Kise kyō*). They closely resemble bees in terms of body structure and hamulate wing system. They appear frequently in modern *anime* and *manga*.

ボストン美術館所蔵 　一銅釜所（断簡）
原文翻刻

まう別所ありなをは銅釜所

といふむかしひとにむまれていけ

るものをなやまし人をくつ

さきむくひよこの地獄？おり

このところか獄卒はみをと

とらくてあかゝねなくまいれて

をとゝ火をたきて　れをい

罪人身分こかれとをりて苦患

しのふかし

ボストン美術館蔵　銅釜所（断簡）
解読文

また別所あり。名をば銅釜所（どうふしょ）
といふ。昔、人に生まれて生け
る物を悩まし、人を苦し
め、報ひにこの地獄に堕つ
この所に獄卒、罪人を
捉へて銅釜に入れて
下に火を炊きて[こ脱力]れを煎[る脱力]
罪人、焦がり通りて苦け悶
忍び難し。

ボストン美術館蔵 『一銅釜所*（断簡）
現代語訳

　もう一つの別所がある。その名を一銅釜所*という。昔、人間として生まれ、生き物を悩ませ、他人を苦しませた人が、報いとしてこの地獄に堕ちる。

　この所では獄卒が罪人を捉え、銅鍋に入れ、その下に火を焚いて、中の罪人を煎る。罪人はこんがりと焼かれ、その苦悩は忍びがたい。

* 『起世経』に説かれる「一銅釜所」を指すと思われる。

MFA, Boston Fragment: The Sub-Hell of One Copper Cauldron

There is yet another sub-hell. As for its name, it is called the "The [Sub-Hell] of the Copper Cauldron*". The ones who descend into this hell for punishment are those who, long ago, when they were born human, harassed living things and caused other people to suffer.

In this place, the demons of hell snatch sinners and put them into a copper pot. They start a fire under the pot and roast the sinners. The sinners are cooked brown all the way through; their suffering is difficult to endure.

* Writing and illustration styles confirm that this fragment was originally part of the Nara Scroll. It is currently held by the Museum of Fine Arts, Boston. This passage refers to the sub-hell of "One Copper Cauldron," which is described in the seventh chapter of the *Sutra on the Origins of the World* (Jp. *Kise kyō*). The MFA, Boston calls the piece "The Burning Cauldron."

東京国立博物館所蔵（東博本）

『地獄草紙』詞書

東博本　第一段　髪火流所（はつかるしょ）　原文翻刻

又この地獄に別所ありなをば

髪火流といふこゝろの衆生むかし

人間よありて殺生倫盗邪婬をよひま

て五戒をそなちたる人のまく了

をてさけをのむて殺て戒を破り

といふてさけをあたくて戒をやぶる

しめすもしものこの地獄をおりこ

のちく〻は鉄鐵のいぬけえ人の

あををくらふ。あるいてまたひのを玟

くろしあつくろかねのわし罪人乃

かうくをけきわりてうのなけきを

まふとつ苦悪をふくから救をけふこ

ゑ門きま

東博本　第一段　髪火流所（はつかるしょ）解読文

また、この地獄に別所あり。名をば髪火流（所脱カ）といふ。この所の衆生、昔、人間にありて、殺生・偸盗・邪淫、及びまた五戒を保ちたる人の前にして、「酒を飲むは、目出度き戒なり」と言ひて、酒を与へて戒を破らしめたりし者、この地獄に堕つ。この地獄には熱鉄の犬、罪人の足を食ふ。或いはまた、炎の嘴ある黒金の鷲、罪人の頭を突き割りてその脳を吸ひ取る。苦患耐ふべからず。叫ぶ声、尽きず。

東博本 第一段 髪火流所 現代語訳

この地獄にもう一つの別所があり、その名を髪火流所という。この所の衆生は昔、人間であり、殺生、窃盗、邪淫を犯し、また五戒*を守っている人の前で「酒を飲むのは目出度い戒めである」と言って、酒を与え、戒を破らせていた者で、(このような人は)この地獄に堕ちる。

この地獄には熱ねった鉄の犬が罪人の足を食う。或いはまた、炎の嘴ばしがある鉄の鷲が罪人の頭を突ついき割り、その脳を吸い取る。その苦患は耐え難く、叫ぶ声が尽きない。

* 「五戒」とは仏教において、在家信者が守るべき基本的な五つの戒律で、不殺生、不偸盗、不邪淫、不妄語、不飲酒である。

Tokyo Scroll, Verse 1: The Sub-Hell of Flaming Torrents of Hair

There is yet another sub-hell within this hell. As for its name, it is called "The [Sub-Hell] of Flaming Torrents of Hair." The beings in this place are those who, long ago, when they were human, engaged in killing, theft, and sexual misconduct; those who caused observers of the five precepts* to break their vows by offering them alcohol, saying "Drinking [alcohol] is an auspicious act." These are the (kinds of) people who fall into this hell.

In this hell, there is a dog of molten iron that eats the legs of sinners. There is also an iron eagle that uses its flaming beak to crack open the heads of sinners and suck out their brains. The agony is unbearable; the screams, never-ending.

* The five precepts of Buddhism are fundamental ethical guidelines for lay practitioners, including abstention from killing, stealing, sexual misconduct, lying, and intoxication.

東博本　第二二段　火末虫所(かまつちゅうしょ)　原文翻刻

又この地獄よ別所ありなをは火
末虫といふこのところの衆生むかし
人間かあるて殺生偸盗邪婬ほよ
ひさけよ水を入れておほくあゑて
うりたりしものこの地獄よたこ
の地獄れけみらとの身よりあまたの
むしいて、かたくをしむらほをや
ふりてうの身をまくらふその
くるしみをのふくから猴　けふこ
ゑく殺

東博本　第二段　火末虫所(かまつちゅうしょ)　解読文

また、この地獄に別所あり。名をば火末虫[所脱力]と言ふ。この所の衆生、昔人間にありて、殺生・偸盗・邪淫、及び、酒に水を入れて多く成して売りたりし者この地獄に堕つ。この地獄の罪人の身より数多の虫、出でて、皮辺・肉業・骨を破りて、その身を吸ひ食らふ。その苦しみ、忍ぶべからず。[さ脱力]けぶ声え耐たへず。

東博本 第二段 火末虫所(かまつちゅうしょ) 現代語訳

この地獄にもう1つの別所があり、その名を火末虫所という。この所の衆生は昔人間であり、殺生・偸盗・邪淫を犯し、また酒に水を入れ、その量を増やして売っていた者で、(このような人は)この地獄に堕ちる。

この地獄の罪人の身から、多数の虫が出て皮膚、死肉、骨を破り、その身を吸い食う。その苦しみは忍ぶ事ができない。叫ぶ声が絶えない。

Tokyo Scroll, Verse 2: The Sub-Hell of Insects at the Tips of Flames

There is yet another sub-hell within this hell. As for its name, it is called "The [Sub-Hell] of Insects at the Tips of Flames." The beings in this place are those who, long ago, when they were human, engaged in killing, theft, and sexual misconduct; those who increased the volume of wine for selling by adulterating it with water. These are the (kinds of) people who fall into this hell.

Many bugs emerge from the bodies of the sinners in this hell, consuming their skin, dead flesh, and bones. The suffering is inescapable; the screams, never-ending.

東博本　第三段　雲火霧所(うんかむしょ)　翻刻文

又このぢごくに別所ありなをば雲火霧
処といふこのところの衆生昔人間よし
て殺生偸盗邪婬だもひまたさけをもて
持戒のおとにあくてをしめて子を
ふれしあるけりはちをあてくて二人
二よこしひほこのしゐとこの地獄よ
おけこのちこよくなかほのおみ
てりあつこ二百肘獄卒罪人をとりて
の猛火のなかよなけい犯罪ありもか
うくよいと犯までやゝとおりてきえうせ
ぬれともたよみかくつよみかくきとまた
やくかくのこときやむこなしとけぶこ
ゑ天をおゝかむ

東博本 第三段 雲火霧処 解読文

また、この地獄に別所あり。名をば雲火霧処と言ふ。この所の衆生、昔、人間にして、殺生・偸盗・邪淫及びまた酒をもて持戒の人に与へて酔はしめて、戯れし悔あり、恥を与へて、心に喜び誇りし人、この地獄に堕つ。この地獄は、中に炎満ちて、厚さ二百肘。獄卒、罪人を捕りて、この猛火の中に投げ入る。罪人、足より頭に至るまで、焼け通りて、消え失せぬれば、また蘇る。蘇ればまた焼く。斯くの如きやむことなし。叫ぶ声、天を響びかす。

東博本 第三段 雲火霧所(うんかむしょ) 現代語訳

この地獄にもう一つの別所(べっしょ)がある。その名を雲火霧所という。この所の衆生(しゅじょう)は昔、人間で、その当時、殺生(せっしょう)、窃盗(せっとう)、邪淫(じゃいん)を犯(おか)し、また酒を持(たも)つ戒(いまし)めの人に与えて酔(よ)わせ、戯(たわむ)れて侮(あなど)り、恥(はじ)をかかせて、心に喜び誇った人はこの地獄に堕(お)ちる。この地獄の中は炎(ほのお)に満ちており、その厚さは二百(にひゃく)肘(ちゅう)*である。そこの獄卒(ごくそつ)が罪人を捕(とら)え、猛火(もうか)の中に投げ入れる。罪人は、足より頭(あたま)に至(いた)るまで、焼(や)け尽くされ、消えてしまえば、また蘇(よみが)える。蘇(よみがえ)れば、また焼(や)かれる。このように止(や)むことない。叫(さけ)ぶ声は天(てん)を響(ひび)かせる。

* 「肘」とは、長さをはかる前近代における単位。人間の肘の関節から中指の先端までの約50センチメートルほどの長さ。

Tokyo Scroll, Verse 3: The Sub-Hell of Cloud-Fire Mist

There is yet another sub-hell within this hell. As for its name, it is called "The [Sub-Hell] of Cloud-Fire Mist." The beings in this place are those who, long ago, at that time when they were human, engaged in killing, theft, and sexual misconduct; those too who gave alcohol to observers of the five precepts to get them drunk and, with playful contempt and prideful glee, brought shame upon them. These are the (kinds of) people who fall into this hell.

This hell is engulfed in flames two hundred cubits* thick. The demons of this hell seize sinners and throw them into the roaring flames. From head to foot, the sinners are burned through. Once vaporized, they are brought back to life. Once brought back, they are burned yet again. It continues like this, unending. The screaming voices reverberate in the heavens.

* One "*chū*" represents the distance from the elbow to the fingertips, similar to the word "cubit." It is about 50cm.

東博本　第四段　雨炎火石所　翻刻文
（前半）

又この地獄に別所ありなをは雨炎火石
といふこのところの衆生むかし人間よにありて
殺生偸盗邪婬およひ又たましきをもの
又つれとう友をさそひて山にいつるを
うしなふさけをもうけてとをくひろき
野をゆかんとまつ人よあたえてのます
の三たもりぬれとさふらしてゆくにと
えきうのときにれをうかゝひてゐひ人

東博本 第四段 雨炎火石所 解読文（前半）

また、この地獄に別所あり。名をば雨炎火石と言ふ。この所の衆生、昔、人間にして殺生・偸盗・邪淫 及び また、少しき御物満つれば、魂を惑はし、心を喪ふ。酒を儲けて遠く広き野を行かんとする人に与へて飲ます。飲み終りぬれば、酔ひ臥して行くこと得ず。その時、これを窺ひて、酔ひ人を

東博本 第四段 雨炎火石所 現代語訳（前半）

この地獄にもう一つの別所がある。その名を雨炎火石所という。この所の衆生は昔、人間であり、その当時、殺生、窃盗、邪淫を犯し、また少しの御物が満ちれば、魂を惑わせ、心を喪う。酒を持って、遠い広野く行こうとする人に与えて飲ませる。飲み終われば、酒に酔って寝てしまい、（広野く）行くことができない。その時、状況を待ち構えて、

Tokyo Scroll, Verse 4: The Sub-Hell of Flaming Rain and Rocks (first half)

There is yet another sub-hell within this hell. As for its name, it is called "The [Sub-Hell] of Flaming Rain and Rocks." The beings in this place are those who, long ago, at that time when they were human, engaged in killing, theft, and sexual misconduct; also those who, when they had had enough, drove their own spirit astray, losing their presence of mind. Bearing alcohol, they gave it to people venturing into broad plains and made them drink. When those people had finished drinking and were intoxicated, they fell asleep and were unable to venture forth. Having waited for this very situation…

東博本 第四段 雨炎火石所(うえんかせきしょ) 翻刻文 (後半)

のもたつあらおつそからものをみあう
といとおあつときにくいのちををちら
のしくこの地獄丁をけこのちにくては
ほのおあるしふのてけ三人をやくう
のとき罪人ちふれらしてわくるにと
まあるいとまたかたあの鉄沸河となく
このかてもあかねのゆ白鑞のゆあつき血
あかましものてなか罪人はねう
このかてのあかあり苦をうくるにと
きとひをいつてあそすまたけふにき
たえ数

東博本 第四段 雨炎火石所(うんえんかせきしょ) 解読文（後半）

の持(も)たる、あらゆる宝物(たからもの)を皆(みな)奪(うば)い取(と)る。ある時(とき)には、命(いのち)をも断(た)ちたりし人(ひと)、この地獄(じごく)に堕(お)つ。この地獄には、炎(ほのお)ある石(いし)降(ふ)りて、罪人(つみびと)を焼(や)く。その時、罪人倒(たお)れ臥(ふ)して逃(に)ぐること[得脱力]ず。或(ある)いは、また河(かわ)あり。熱沸(あつふつ)が河(かわ)と名(な)つく。この河に、銅(あかがね)の湯(ゆ)、白鑞(しろなまり)*の湯、熱(あつ)き血(ち)相(あい)交(まじ)わりて流(なが)る。罪人、常(つね)にこの河の中にありて、苦(く)を受(う)くること、譬(たと)ひを取(と)るに能(あた)はず。叫(さけ)ぶ声(こえ)絶(た)えず。

*「白鑞」とは奈良時代おける工芸材料としての錫(すず)を指す。

東博本 第四段 雨炎火石所 現代語訳（後半）

酔った人が持っているあらゆる宝物をすべて奪い取る。ある時には、（酔った人の）命をも絶っていた人がこの地獄に堕ちる。この地獄には、炎の石が振り、罪人を焼く。その時、罪人は倒れて、逃げることができない。或いは、また河がある。名は熱仏河*という。この河に、銅の湯、錫の湯、熱い血が混ざり合い流れる。罪人は常にこの河の中にいて、苦患の受けようは例えようがない。叫び声が絶えない。

* 「熱仏河」とは、地獄を流れるべタラニー河（梵語 Vaitaraṇī Nadī）のことであろう。

Tokyo Scroll, Verse 4: The Sub-Hell of Flaming Rain and Rocks (second half)

...they took that opportunity to rob the intoxicated people of their every treasure. Sometimes, those who fall into this hell have even taken their own lives.

In this hell, flaming rocks rain down and burn the sinners. When this happens, the sinners collapse and are unable to flee.

There is also a river. Its name is the Vaitarṇī River*. It flows with a mixture of molten copper, tin, and hot blood. The sinners remain immersed in this river and are subjected to an incomparable agony. Their screams are never-ending.

* The original text refers literally to the "Hot Buddha River." Although that name does not appear in mainstream sutras or Hindu-Buddhist cosmology, the river's description matches that of the mythical Vaitaraṇī Nadī.

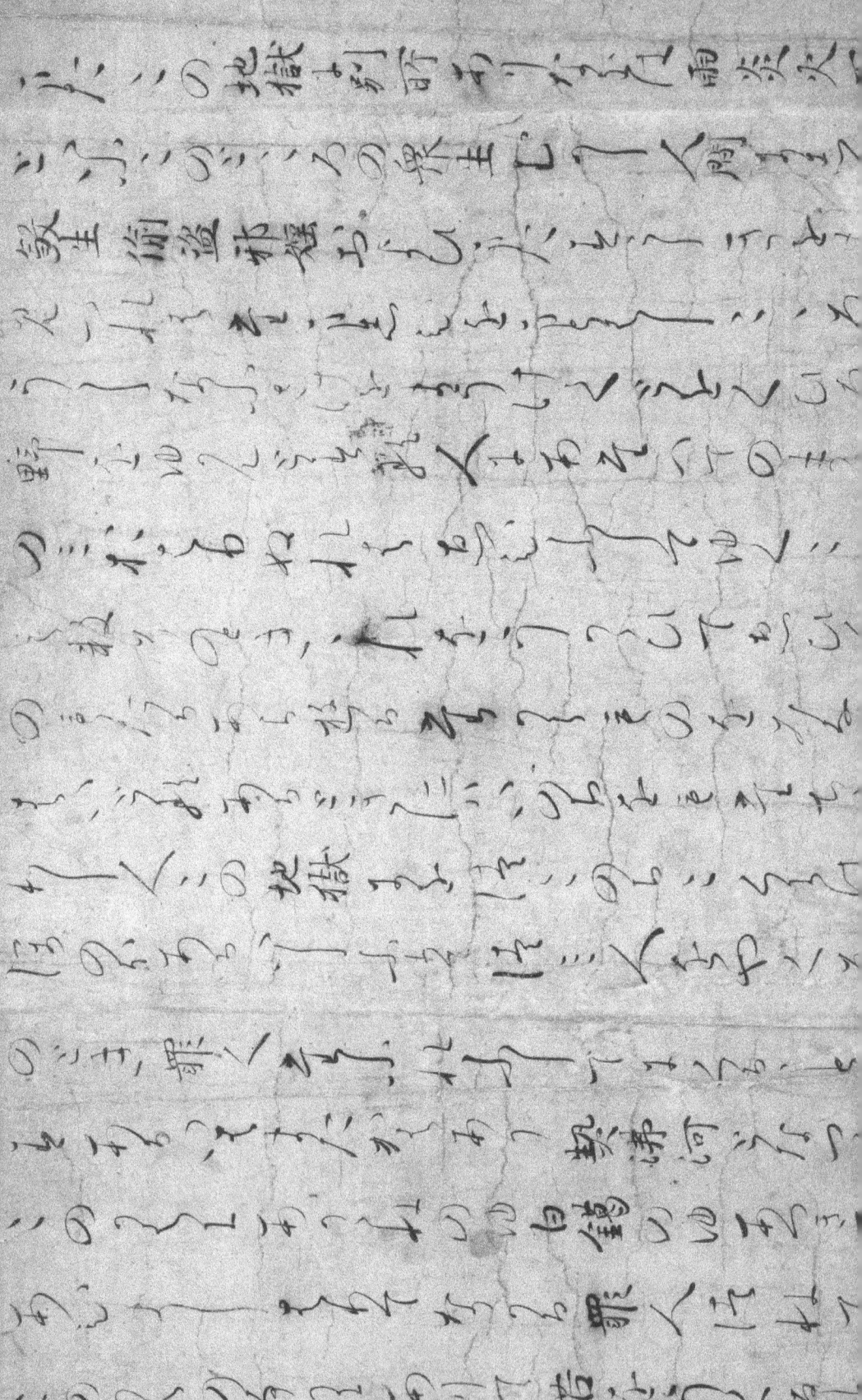

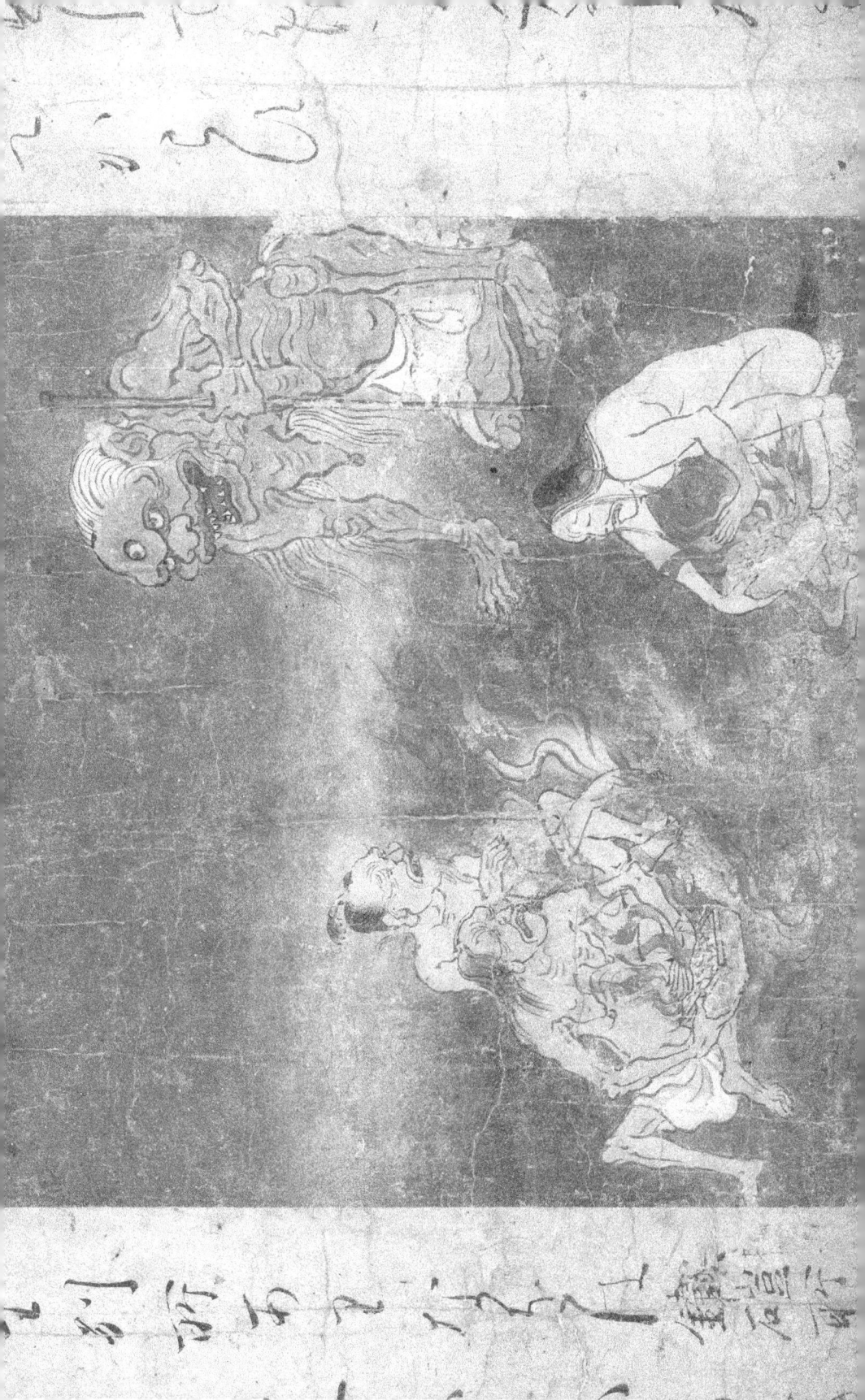

Vicus Lusorum

地獄草紙　詞書 　全文翻刻・解読・現代語訳・英訳

奈良国立博物館所蔵本
ボストン美術館所蔵断簡
東京国立博物館所蔵本

マシュー・スタブロス　監修・翻訳
ジェマイマ・ライス　英文校訂

Hell Scrolls: A complete transcription and translation of *Jigokuzōshi*, the *Hell Scrolls* in the collections of the Nara National Museum and the Tokyo National Museum, including a fragment from the Nara Scroll in the collection of the Museum of Fine Arts, Boston.

Edited, transcribed, and translated into Modern Japanese and English by Matthew Stavros, Ph.D.
Editorial collaboration from Jemima Rice

Copyright © 2025 by Matthew Stavros
30 29 28 27 26 25　　6 5 4 3 2 1
Japan–Art History–Buddhism–Illustrated Scrolls–Translation

All rights reserved. No part of this publication may be reproduced, distributed, or transmitted in any form or by any means, including photocopying, recording, or other electronic or mechanical methods, without the written permission of the publisher, except in the case of brief quotations embedded in critical reviews, academic studies, and certain other non-commercial uses permitted by copyright law.

ISBN: 978-0-6453932-9-3

www.vicuslusorum.com/hell-scrolls
admin@vicuslusorum.com